Half Truths
Leader Guide

Half Truths:
God Helps Those Who Help Themselves and Other Things the Bible Doesn't Say

Half Truths
978-1-5018-1387-0
978-1-5018-1388-7 eBook
978-1-5018-1389-4 Large Print
Audiobook available on Audible

Half Truths: DVD
978-1-5018-1392-4

Half Truths: Leader Guide
978-1-5018-1390-0
978-1-5018-1391-7 eBook

Half Truths:
Youth Study Book
978-1-5018-1398-6
978-1-5018-1399-3 eBook

Half Truths:
Youth Leader Guide
978-1-5018-1400-6
978-1-5018-1401-3 eBook

For more information, visit www.AdamHamilton.org.

Also by Adam Hamilton

24 Hours That Changed the World
Christianity and World Religions
Christianity's Family Tree
Confronting the Controversies
Enough
Final Words from the Cross
Forgiveness
John
Leading Beyond the Walls
Love to Stay
Making Sense of the Bible
Not a Silent Night

Revival
Seeing Gray in a World of
  Black and White
Selling Swimsuits in the Arctic
Speaking Well
The Call
The Journey
The Way
Unleashing the Word
When Christians Get It Wrong
Why?

ADAM HAMILTON

Author of *24 Hours That Changed the World, The Journey,* and *The Way*

HALF
TRUTHS

GOD HELPS THOSE WHO HELP THEMSELVES
AND OTHER THINGS THE BIBLE DOESN'T SAY

Leader Guide
by Martha Bettis Gee

Abingdon Press / Nashville

Half Truths
God Helps Those Who Help Themselves
and Other Things the Bible Doesn't Say
Leader Guide

This book is printed on elemental chlorine-free paper.
ISBN 978-1-5018-1390-0

16 17 18 19 20 21 22 23 24 25 — 10 9 8 7 6 5 4 3 2 1
MANUFACTURED IN THE UNITED STATES OF AMERICA

CONTENTS

TO THE LEADER

Welcome! In this study, you have the opportunity to help a group of learners as they explore some familiar and popular ideas that many Christians proclaim and believe to be true.

Jesus Christ said, "I am the way, the truth, and the life." He also proclaimed that the truth will set us free. As Christians, we believe that our faith is about truth. Yet Adam Hamilton, the author of this study, contends that there are some ideas Christians embrace that may not be entirely true. Some of these ideas that we may claim and proclaim have the ring of truth. They may even be partially supported by Scripture (although some are not even in the Bible). But when examined closely, we come to discover that these are half truths at best. At worst, despite our best intentions, they can be stumbling blocks, both for those of us who use them and for those to whom we address these ideas. When we speak half truths, we may not only effectively deny the authenticity of others' experiences, we may also avoid the hard work of grappling with complex issues and painful realities, to the detriment of our faith life.

Scripture tells us that where two or three are gathered together, we can be assured of the Holy Spirit's presence, working in and through all those gathered. As you prepare to lead, pray for that presence and expect that you will experience it.

The study includes five sessions. It makes use of the following components:

- Adam Hamilton's book *Half Truths: God Helps Those Who Help Themselves and Other Things the Bible Doesn't Say*;
- the DVD that accompanies the study;
- this Leader Guide.

Participants in the study will also need Bibles, as well as a way to journal, perhaps with a spiral-bound notebook or an electronic tablet. If possible, notify those interested in the study before the first session. Make arrangements for them to get copies of the book so that they can read the Introduction and Chapter 1.

Using This Guide with Your Group

Because no two groups are alike, this guide has been designed to give you flexibility and choice in tailoring the sessions for your group. The session format is listed below. You may choose any or all of the activities, adapting them as you wish to meet the schedule and needs of your particular group.

The leader guide offers a basic session plan designed to be completed in about forty-five minutes. In addition, you will find two or more extra activities that are optional. You may decide to add these activities or substitute them for those suggested in the basic plan. Select ahead of time which activities your group will do, for how long, and in what order. Depending on which activities you select, there may be special preparation needed. The leader is alerted in the session plan when advance preparation is needed.

Session Format

Planning the Session

    Session Goals
    Biblical Foundation
    Special Preparation

Getting Started

    Opening Activity
    Opening Prayer

Learning Together

    Video and Discussion
    Bible Study and Discussion
    Book Study and Discussion
    More Activities (optional)

Wrapping Up

    Closing Activity
    Closing Prayer

Helpful Hints

Preparing for the Session

- Pray for the leading of the Holy Spirit as you prepare for the study. Pray for discernment for yourself and for each member of the study group.
- Before each session, familiarize yourself with the content. Read the book chapter again.
- Choose the session elements you will use during the group session, including the specific discussion questions you plan

to cover. Be prepared, however, to adjust the session as group members interact and as questions arise. Prepare carefully, but allow space for the Holy Spirit to move in and through the group members and through you as facilitator.

- Prepare the room where the group will meet so that the space will enhance the learning process. Ideally, group members should be seated around a table or in a circle so that all can see one another. Movable chairs are best, because the group will often be forming pairs or small groups for discussion.
- Bring a supply of Bibles for those who forget to bring their own. Some sessions use a variety of translations. If you don't have access to different translations, you can find many translations of a particular passage at a website such as BibleGateway.com.
- Also bring writing paper and pens for those participants who do not bring a notebook or tablet or electronic means of journaling.
- For most sessions you will also need either a chalkboard and chalk, a whiteboard and markers, or an easel with paper and markers.

Shaping the Learning Environment

- Begin and end on time.
- Create a climate of openness, encouraging group members to participate as they feel comfortable.
- For some participants, examining as half truths several statements they may have embraced and used routinely may present a distinct challenge. Others may have experienced trauma, adversity, or painful experiences with which they might have struggled to reconcile with a loving and caring God. Some of these statements may have been addressed to them by well-meaning Christians. Be on the lookout for signs of discomfort or uncertainty in those who may be

silent, and encourage them to express their thoughts and feelings honestly.

- Remember that some people will jump right in with answers and comments, while others need time to process what is being discussed.

- If you notice that some group members don't enter the conversation, ask them if they have thoughts to share. Give everyone a chance to talk, but keep the conversation moving. Moderate the discussion to prevent a few individuals from doing all the talking.

- Communicate the importance of group discussions and group exercises.

- If no one answers at first during discussions, do not be afraid of silence. Count silently to ten, then say something such as, "Would anyone like to go first?" If no one responds, venture an answer yourself and ask for comments.

- Model openness as you share with the group. Group members will follow your example. If you limit your sharing to a surface level, others will follow suit.

- Encourage multiple answers or responses before moving on.

- To help continue a discussion and give it greater depth, ask, "Why?" or "Why do you believe that?" or "Can you say more about that?"

- Affirm others' responses with comments such as "Great" or "Thanks" or "Good insight," especially if it's the first time someone has spoken during the group session.

- Monitor your own contributions. If you are doing most of the talking, back off so that you do not train the group to listen rather than speak up.

- Remember that you do not have all the answers. Your job is to keep the discussion going and encourage participation.

Managing the Session

- Honor the time schedule. If a session is running longer than expected, get consensus from the group before continuing beyond the agreed-upon ending time.
- Involve group members in various aspects of the group session, such as saying prayers or reading Scripture.
- Note that the session guides sometimes call for breaking into smaller groups or pairs. This gives everyone a chance to speak and participate fully. Mix up the groups; don't let the same people pair up for every activity.
- As always in discussions that may involve personal sharing, confidentiality is essential. Group members should never pass along stories that have been shared in the group. Remind the group members at each session: confidentiality is crucial to the success of this study.

1.

EVERYTHING HAPPENS FOR A REASON

Planning the Session

Session Goals

As a result of conversations and activities connected with this session, group members should begin to:

- examine the ways this half truth does not capture the truth of the Bible;
- embrace an understanding of a sovereign God who gives freedom and works through people for good.

Biblical Foundation

[Then Moses said to the Israelites,] "I call heaven and earth to witness against you today that I have set before you life and death,

blessings and curses. Choose life so that you and your descendants
may live, loving the LORD your God, obeying him, and holding
fast to him; for that means life to you and length of days."

—Deuteronomy 30:19-20a NRSV

Special Preparation

- In advance of the session, cut some newspaper clippings or
  download and print current Internet news stories about
  disasters resulting from weather events, crimes such as mass
  shootings, upheavals resulting in mass migrations of refugees,
  and the like. Have available enough stories for every two
  anticipated participants. Following the session, collect these
  news accounts from participants and set them aside to revisit
  in Session 3.
- On a large sheet of paper or a board, print John Wesley's
  Covenant Prayer, included at the end of the book chapter
  but also below as the closing prayer for this session.
- Decide if you will do any of the optional activities. For
  "Picturing God," you will need four large sheets of paper and
  colored markers. For "Explore the Concept of Dominion,"
  you will need a large sheet of paper or a board and a marker
  and several versions of the Bible.

Getting Started

Opening Activity

As group members arrive, welcome them to the study. If anyone did
not bring a notebook or an electronic device such as a tablet or laptop
for journaling, provide a notebook or paper and pen or pencil.

Gather together. If group members are not familiar with one another,
provide nametags and allow a few moments for introductions. Form
pairs and distribute a news account to each pair. Allow a minute or

two for pairs to read over their accounts. In the large group, invite one or two volunteers briefly to summarize the information in their account, describing the event and what happened as a result.

On a large piece of paper or a board, print "Everything happens for a reason." Ask participants to indicate with a show of hands if they have ever had someone say this to them, or if they themselves have said it. Then ask them to consider in silence the following:

- How, if at all, do I believe the events in my news account fit into God's plan?

Call the group's attention to the book introduction. If they have not already read it, ask them to scan the information quickly. Ask:

- How does Adam Hamilton define biblical half truths?

Tell the group that in this study, they will have the opportunity to examine five popular statements that, though we may accept them as truth, actually represent half truths. Today's session addresses the statement, "Everything happens for a reason."

Opening Prayer

Gracious God, we yearn for deeper insights into your loving intent for humankind. We struggle to reconcile the difficult and painful parts of living with a God who loves us and desires an abundant life for us. Guide us as we seek to better understand your truth. Amen.

Learning Together

Video Study and Discussion

Briefly introduce Adam Hamilton, the book author and video presenter. Adam Hamilton is senior pastor of The United Methodist

Church of the Resurrection in Leawood, Kansas. He writes and teaches on life's tough questions, the doubts with which we all wrestle, and the challenging issues we face today. He likes to explore the "gray" areas that present themselves between the Bible's teachings and our life experiences. Participants can learn more about Hamilton and his other books at www.AdamHamilton.org.

Adam Hamilton introduces us to statements many Christians commonly use that he suggests are actually half truths. The first half truth he discusses is "Everything happens for a reason."

- What are some situations you can name where you or someone else, responded by asserting that everything happens for a reason?
- Hamilton points out similar aphorisms: "It's all part of God's plan" or "It was God's will." How do you respond to the understanding that painful, tragic, or evil occurrences are a part of God's plan for the world?
- What does Hamilton say about how sovereigns operate in ruling their people? How does this help us understand the sovereignty of God?
- Hamilton suggests that we need to be attentive to the whisper of God's voice in making us aware of what needs to be done. Can you name a time when you responded to a nudge from God?

Bible Study and Discussion

Invite a volunteer to read aloud the session's Scripture focus, Deuteronomy 30:19-20a, which is shown above and at the beginning of book Chapter 1. Set the scene for the scripture: through Moses, God has led the Israelites out of slavery in Egypt, where they have wandered for forty years. As they prepare to enter the Promised Land, Moses, an old man facing death, reiterates the law for the people and reminds them of God's expectations. Ask:

- What are the choices Moses lays before the people?
- What do these choices imply to you about the statement "Everything happens for a reason"?

Book Study and Discussion

Review Critiques

If they have not already done so, ask participants to read over quickly the information in the first five paragraphs of the book chapter. Note that three critiques are offered of the idea that everything happens for a reason. Form small groups of three. In each group, assign to each person one of the three critiques of the idea that are offered. Ask participants to read over briefly the information in the chapter about their assigned critique. Then ask each group member to summarize that critique for the other two in the group. Back in the large group, ask participants to discuss the following:

- What implications does Hamilton suggest about each critique?
- Does each of the three critiques make sense to you? If not, why?

Revisit the news accounts from the opening activity. Ask volunteers to explain how the view that everything happens for a reason applies to the events in the news. Encourage them to evaluate each event using one or more of the critiques in the book chapter.

Explore Contrasting Views

Ask volunteers to define briefly the theological concepts of God's providence and sovereignty. Point out the contrasting ways in which Christians interpret these two concepts: some picture God as micromanager, while others view God as an absentee landlord. If they have not already done so, invite the group to scan the information quickly under the heading "Calvinism and Theological Determinism." Discuss some of the following:

- How did John Calvin understand the sovereignty of God?
- What was Calvin's understanding of how the grace of God operates?
- The concept of predestination has experienced a recent resurgence. What does Hamilton suggest is the reason that many people have embraced this concept? Does his explanation make sense to you? Why or why not?
- What do you think about Hamilton's understanding of how God operates? Are there problems you can identify in this view? If so, what?
- How can we reconcile the concept of predestination with the understanding that humankind has dominion over creation? Or with the understanding that we have been created with the capacity for making choices?

Invite the group to review the information under the heading "Deism and the Hands-Off God." Discuss some of the following:

- How does Hamilton define deism? What does he identify as the problem with this view of God?
- He observes that God does sometimes intervene in the affairs of this world in miraculous ways. Would you agree? Why or why not? Can you name an event that you consider to represent a miraculous intervention?
- What does Hamilton suggest we do to make ourselves receptive to God's working in and through us?
- Have you ever experienced God's nudges in your life? If so, how, and in what circumstances? How did you respond?

Call the attention of participants to the information under the heading, "God Is Sovereign, Gives Freedom, and Works Through

People." Note the Facebook meme that begins, "Everything happens for a reason, but…" Based on their reading of the text, invite volunteers to complete the meme with their own endings. Discuss the following:

- Hamilton observes that in looking back on the most painful experiences of his life, he can see how God used them to bring about something good and beautiful. What do you think of this view? Has this been your experience, or not?

More Activities (Optional)

Picturing God

Form two smaller groups. Give each group a large sheet of paper and colored markers. Assign to one group the image of God as micromanager and to the other group the image of God as absentee landlord. Ask each group to flesh out their assigned image, illustrating the image by drawing what this God would look like, or by using symbols, words, or phrases to illustrate it. After allowing a few minutes for groups to work, ask them to show their work and describe how this God would act. Discuss:

- If God can be described as a micromanager, what is the role of human beings in their relationship to God?
- If God is like an absentee landlord, what is our role, and how do we relate to God?

Then ask the group to describe a sovereign God who gives freedom and works through people. Invite both groups to illustrate this God on another large sheet of paper, using drawings, words, or phrases.

Explore the Concept of Dominion

Distribute to participants several different versions of the Bible (or download and print several versions of Genesis 1 from a website such

as www.BibleGateway.com). Invite volunteers to read aloud Genesis
1:26-28 from their assigned version. On a large sheet of paper or a
board, print the words used in each version for "have dominion over."
Discuss:

- Hamilton believes we have been given the gift of dominion.
  What does that communicate to you? Are there other words
  from other translations that expand or amplify that meaning
  for you?
- He says that part of what it means to be human is the
  freedom to choose our own actions. How do you respond to
  that? What advantages or disadvantages does it suggest?
- Hamilton also notes that even amoral decisions—those that
  are not moral decisions—have consequences. He gives as an
  example his love of riding a motorcycle, with the attendant
  freedom to risk injury or death. What examples from your
  own life could conceivably result in consequences to yourself
  or others?

Engage in a Deeper Exploration of Theological Determinism

Engage the group in a "fishbowl discussion" as a way to examine
theological determinism in John Calvin's thought. Place four chairs
in the center of the room. Give participants a few minutes to read
over the description of Calvin's thought in the book chapter. Ask for a
volunteer to take the role of John Calvin. Then ask two other volunteers to take the roles of people who have questions for Calvin about
his views. Seat these three people in the chairs. Tell the rest of the
group that at any time, they can take the fourth chair in order to join
the discussion, ask a question, or raise a point, then they will get up so
someone else can take the seat. After allowing a few minutes for the
roleplay, debrief with the group. Discuss:

- Calvin believed that everything that happens is fixed by God's decree. How do you reconcile this view with the idea of humanity's free will?
- How do you respond to the idea that you were predestined to be among the elect, or not? If you believe this, how might it affect the way you live your life?

Wrapping Up

Closing Activity

Invite participants to make observations or raise lingering questions they may have about the "half truth" that everything happens for a reason.

Recall for the group that in the opening activity they discussed whether they had ever had someone say to them "Everything happens for a reason" or if they themselves had ever said it. Ask:

- What were the circumstances when someone said it to you, or when you yourself said it? What additional thoughts or feelings do you have about the expression following this group session?

Note that often this half truth is elicited in painful situations, where someone is suffering because of a loss or deep disappointment. Ask a volunteer to read from the book the quotation retired pastor Ray Firestone shared about suffering. Ask someone else to read from the book the words written by the mother of the boy named Austin, regarding what happened to her son and how it affected her faith. Ask:

- In a time of suffering or sorrow, if you had had the opportunity to offer different words, or to hear them, what would those words be?

- How would you attempt to frame a response reflecting a deeper understanding of God's sovereignty, human freedom, and the consequences of our choices?

Encourage participants to note these questions in their journals and reflect on them in the coming week. Also ask that they read Chapter 2 before the next session.

Closing Prayer

Chapter 1 closes with John Wesley's Covenant Prayer, a prayer of surrender used by British Methodists in a covenant service on the first weekend of the New Year. Invite the group to join you in offering this prayer together:

I am no longer my own, but thine.
Put me to what thou wilt, rank me with whom thou wilt.
Put me to doing, put me to suffering.
Let me be employed for thee or laid aside for thee,
exalted for thee or brought low for thee.
Let me be full, let me be empty.
Let me have all things, let me have nothing.
I freely and heartily yield all things to thy pleasure and disposal.
And now, O glorious and blessed God,
Father, Son, and Holy Spirit,
thou art mine, and I am thine.
So be it.
And the covenant which I have made on earth,
let it be ratified in heaven. Amen.

2.

GOD HELPS THOSE WHO HELP THEMSELVES

Planning the Session

Session Goals

As a result of conversations and activities connected with this session, group members should begin to:

- examine the ways this half truth does not capture the truth of the Bible;
- embrace an understanding of a loving God who helps us even when we cannot help ourselves.

Biblical Foundation

The helpless commit themselves to you; you have been the helper of the orphan.... O LORD, you will hear the desire of the meek; you will strengthen their heart, you will incline your ear to do justice for the orphan and the oppressed.

—*Psalm 10:14b, 17-18a NRSV*

In my distress I called upon the LORD; to my God I cried for help. From his temple he heard my voice, and my cry to him reached his ears.... He reached down from on high, he took me; he drew me out of mighty waters.

—*Psalm 18:6, 16 NRSV*

I lift up my eyes to the hills—from where will my help come? My help comes from the LORD, who made heaven and earth.

—*Psalm 121:1-2 NRSV*

Special Preparation

- On a large sheet of paper or a board, print the following:
  o Pray about it.
  o Prepare a résumé.
  o Network with friends and former colleagues who know my skill set.
  o Actively look for job openings online.
  o Submit applications, along with a cover letter, to indicate my skills and qualifications.
  o Prepare for interviews by dressing well and researching the company.
- If you choose to do an optional activity, gather the necessary materials. For both activities, participants may need writing paper and pens (or they may use their journals to take notes). For the activity "Go Beyond Thoughts and Prayers," you will need a large piece of paper or a board and markers.

Getting Started

Opening Activity

Welcome group members and introduce any who are new to the group. Form pairs, and ask pairs to generate quickly a list of the Ten Commandments without referring to their Bibles or smartphones. After allowing a minute or two, ask each pair to name a commandment until all ten have been named. Then call the group's attention to the fact that in the beginning of Chapter 2, Adam Hamilton recalls a segment of *The Tonight Show* in which Jay Leno asked people on the street to name one of the Ten Commandments. Ask:

- What "commandment" that is not a commandment did many people name? (God helps those who help themselves.)

Tell participants that in this session they will examine this common saying, often erroneously thought to be in the Bible, and explore some ways in which it is true, as well as some other ways in which it is absolutely untrue.

Opening Prayer

God, we give thanks that you are always with us, sustaining us with your love. Be with us now as we seek to discern the deeper truth of your Word. In the name of Jesus Christ, who became flesh and dwelt among us. Amen.

Learning Together

Video Study and Discussion

Adam Hamilton explores the saying "God helps those who help themselves," which is often erroneously thought to be in the Bible.

- When people use that statement, what do you think they intend to convey? In your opinion, what do they convey?
- How do people exemplify the idea of praying and working in the blessing of food at a meal? What must happen in order for the meal to be available?
- Hamilton suggests there are ways in which the statement "God helps those who help themselves" is not true. What are those ways, and how might they be misleading or hurtful to others?
- Hamilton notes that sometimes people are simply unable to help themselves. In what circumstances have you felt unable to cope on your own? How was God's grace manifested to you in those situations?

Bible Study and Discussion

Invite volunteers to read aloud the three excerpts from the Psalms that are the foundation for this session: Psalm 10:14, 17–18; Psalm 18:6, 16; and Psalm 121:1-2. (These excerpts can be found above or in the book at the beginning of Chapter 2.) Ask:

- Have you ever found yourself in a situation that you felt you were helpless to alleviate or stop? Describe the situation and how you felt.
- Did you turn to God for help? How did you pray, and what was the outcome?

Invite one or two volunteers to describe their experience. Ask group members to reflect on times in their own lives or the lives of others when it seemed that despair and hopelessness might win out and there seemed to be nowhere to turn but to God—times, in other words, when helping themselves was simply not an option. Tell the group that in this session they will be considering this experience and reflecting on what it means for our faith.

Book Study and Discussion

Consider Praying and Working

Point out that although the statement "God helps those who help themselves" is not in the Bible and represents at best a partial truth, the statement does hint at one important truth. Invite participants to read the steps you posted that might be taken by someone in a job search. (See Special Preparation above.) Invite group members to indicate with a show of hands any and all steps they themselves might take in a search for employment. Then ask:

- On a job search, how many of you would simply pray about it, then sit back and wait for God to provide a job?
- In situations like this, do you think God expects us to rely only on prayer? Why or why not?

Ask group members to name other situations in which simply praying for God's help will not suffice. Encourage them to give reasons why in these cases prayer itself is insufficient.

Ask a volunteer to read aloud 2 Thessalonians 3:10-12, the excerpt from Paul's letter to the Christians at Thessalonika that is included in the chapter. Ask the group to describe the context of this passage that is given in the text. Discuss:

- How and why were the Thessalonians mistakenly interpreting what it meant to trust in Jesus?
- What was their understanding of how God provided for their needs? What is your understanding of how God provides for you?

Invite group members to give the meaning of the phrase *ora et labora*. Then ask a volunteer to summarize the story of the 1965 civil rights march in Selma, Alabama, an event that came to be known as "Bloody Sunday." Discuss:

- How did civil rights activists live out their understanding of "pray and work"?
- What do you think was the responsibility of Christians at that time to work for the civil rights of others?
- What current problems in the life of our community, nation, and world do you think call for Christians to pray and work for justice?
- The civil rights activists of the 1960s were willing to sacrifice and even to risk death in order to bring about a more just society. For what current problems do you think you would be willing to take risks in order to effect change?
- Hamilton states that our times of prayer can empower us for and guide us into action. Do you agree? How does your prayer life function in times such as this?

Explore Two Key Considerations

Hamilton notes there are two important senses in which the idea that God helps those who help themselves is theologically wrong and fundamentally unbiblical. Form two smaller groups, and assign to each group one of the following: "God's Concern for the Poor and Needy" and "God's Help for the Helpless = Grace." Ask each group to read quickly about their assigned topic and be prepared to argue that the statement "God helps those who help themselves" is neither biblically nor theologically true. Group members should prepare to give examples that Hamilton cites from his own experience and from the Bible, as well as examples from their own experience where applicable. Back in the large group, ask each smaller group to report. If the following questions have not already emerged from group presentations, discuss them together now.

About God's concern for those who are poor and in need:

- Hamilton contends that God is not requiring us to share our wealth, because it is not ours to begin with. What does he mean? How do you respond to this idea?
- Would you agree that compassion for others is a form of worship? Why or why not?
- Hamilton cautions that in helping others, we should be careful to aid in their independence and not make them more dependent. What are some of the ways we can do this?
- In your opinion, how is compassion connected to justice? What can you suggest as ways of demonstrating compassion while still working to transform unjust systems?

About God's grace:

- We receive blessings from God even when we cannot earn them and do not deserve them. This idea is directly counter to the idea that God helps those who help themselves. What has been your experience in this regard? How do you respond to these two ideas?
- All of us have two kinds of needs: the basics of life and higher level needs. In your view, how does God call us to help others meet their basic needs, such as food, clothing, and shelter? How are we called to partner with God in helping others attain their higher needs?
- Other than through people, what means or agency does Hamilton say God uses in intervening directly to help us? What means or agency, if any, do you say God uses in intervening?

More Activities (Optional)

Hold a Debate

Hold a variation on a debate about the statement "God helps those who help themselves." Instead of debating whether the statement is true or false, form two groups to present key reasons as to why the statement is only a partial truth at best. Assign to one group the idea of God's concern for people who are poor or in need, and assign to the other group the concept of God's help for the helpless. Allow time for each group to present its argument, as well as for the other group to pose questions. Debrief the exercise together, encouraging comments and observations.

Go Beyond Thoughts and Prayers

On a board or large piece of paper, print the words "Our thoughts and prayers are with you." Point out to participants that when there is a tragedy, these words are often given verbally, posted on Facebook, or included in sympathy cards. Invite participants to give examples of tragedies, then divide into several smaller groups, each of which should select one of the examples. Encourage the groups to discuss the following in relation to the example chosen:

- What steps should a person take in order to be God's instrument of comfort and transformation in this situation?
- What steps would not be helpful in this situation, and why? (Recall Hamilton's ineffective efforts to help a person experiencing homelessness.) In this situation, what is the value of listening?
- Beyond prayer and actions of mercy and comfort, does this situation involve systemic problems that need to be addressed before healing can take place? What are some of those problems and possible solutions?
- What risks might be involved for those who work for justice in this situation?

Allow time for the smaller groups to report to the large group. Encourage participants to continue reflecting on how God might work through them and to think twice before merely saying or posting this routine statement in the face of tragedy.

Wrapping Up

Closing Activity

Invite participants to make observations or raise lingering questions about the partial truth that God helps those who help themselves. Invite them to reflect in their journals during the coming week on the following:

- How is God calling me to work to transform the world?
- How can my prayer life empower me and guide me into action?

Ask that they read Chapter 3 before the next session.

Invite the group to recall Hamilton's examples of people who were unable to help themselves (the unemployed person who received an anonymous gift of money, the woman at the hotel whose credit card was declined, the couple who lost their teenage son, the couple struggling with the husband's sex addiction). Encourage the group to name the people in each of these examples who served as God's instruments of grace.

Invite participants to keep these examples in mind, as well as situations in their own lives that might involve powerlessness in difficult situations. Then read aloud the following words of the Apostle Paul:

> *Don't be anxious about anything; rather, bring up all of your requests to God in your prayers and petitions, along with giving thanks. Then the peace of God that exceeds all understanding will keep your hearts and minds safe in Christ Jesus.*
>
> *(Philippians 4:6-7)*

Closing Prayer

Remind the group that, though praying about a situation may not be all that is needed, prayer can empower us and guide us into action. We are also called to pray continually for discernment. Offer the following prayer, adapted from the closing prayer at the end of Chapter 2. Tell the group that you will pause for times of silence during the prayer and encourage them to offer their own thanks to God for particular situations when they have cried out to God and have received comfort.

God, thank you for grace. Thank you for the many times you have helped us when we did not deserve it. (Pause for a time of silence.)

Thank you for your love. Thank you for your forgiveness. Thank you for the meaning you bring to our lives. Thank you for rescuing us. (Pause for a time of silence.)

Please use us, Lord, as your instrument to help others who are in need. We offer ourselves to you in Jesus' name. Amen.

3.

GOD WON'T GIVE YOU MORE THAN YOU CAN HANDLE

Planning the Session

Session Goals

As a result of conversations and activities connected with this session, group members should begin to:

- examine the ways this half truth does not capture the truth of the Bible;
- embrace an understanding of a God who helps people find a way through temptation and hard times, and who brings others to stand with those in need and to surround them with love and care.

Biblical Foundation

No temptation has seized you that isn't common for people. But God is faithful. He won't allow you to be tempted beyond your abilities. Instead, with the temptation, God will also supply a way out so that you will be able to endure it.

—*1 Corinthians 10:13*

God is our refuge and strength, a help always near in times of great trouble. That's why we won't be afraid when the world falls apart.

—*Psalm 46:1-2*

Special Preparation

- In advance, make two signs, labeled "Very helpful" and "Very unhelpful." Place these two signs on opposite sides of your learning space.
- Have available for this session the news accounts from Session 1. If you like, add more news accounts of catastrophic events that have occurred since the first session.
- If you decide to do an optional activity, gather the necessary materials. For "Consider Idols that Tempt," you will need drawing paper and colored markers or crayons for participants. For "Create Poetry" and "Experience the Lord's Prayer," you will need large sheets of paper or a board and markers, and the participants will need their journals.
- It is likely that one or more people in the group may be struggling with some kind of adversity or a painful situation. Try to provide an atmosphere that allows those people to articulate the pain of those experiences or opt out of disclosing them to the group, as they choose.

Getting Started

Opening Activity

Welcome group members and introduce any who are new to the group. Gather together.

Invite the group to listen as you read the following from the book *Half Truths*:

> I know you're going through a tough time right now. You feel like you're sinking. The burden is too heavy. You don't know how much more you can bear. But it's going to be all right. You're going to make it through. Remember, God never gives us more than we can handle.

Ask group members to think about situations in their own lives, either past or present, that have been difficult or painful. Point out the two signs you posted on opposite sides of your learning space. With those experiences in mind, invite group members to line up along a continuum according to how helpful they would have found the words you just read in providing comfort.

When all participants have found a position along the continuum that best expresses their feelings, invite one or two participants to describe briefly the experiences they have in mind and why they placed themselves where they did on the continuum. If participants don't feel comfortable disclosing an adverse situation from their ives, simply ask them to reflect on whether they have found words such as this helpful, and why or why not.

Tell the group that in this session they will be examining the biblical and theological veracity of the statement "God won't give you more than you can handle."

Opening Prayer

Pray the following, or a prayer of your choosing:

Faithful God, we give thanks for your presence in our good times and our bad times. Guide us as we explore more deeply your nature and your enduring love for us. In the name of Jesus Christ, who knew what it is to be human. Amen.

Learning Together

Video Study and Discussion

Adam Hamilton explores the half truth "God won't give you more than you can handle." He describes ways in which the saying is true, along with ways in which the saying is untrue and may be a misinterpretation of Scripture.

- Hamilton states that God is not testing you through difficult circumstances to see how much you can handle, but instead God promises to help you handle all that you've been given. By what means does Hamilton suggest God comes alongside us in those situations?
- Hamilton observes that the promise of Scripture is not that we will never experience dark and difficult times. What then is the promise of Scripture? When have you experienced painful and difficult times, and how has God helped you?
- How, if at all, does changing the position of the punctuation in the Lord's Prayer as Hamilton suggests alter its meaning for you?

Bible Study and Discussion

Invite a volunteer to read the first of today's focus scriptures, 1 Corinthians 10:13 (found above and at the beginning of book

Chapter 3). Adam Hamilton tells us that this verse is often cited as the scriptural basis for today's half truth, but in fact when used in this way it has been taken out of context and given a different meaning from what Paul intended. Ask the group to read silently the surrounding text—1 Corinthians 10:1–22—then read Hamilton's comments under the heading "Context and Origin." Invite a volunteer or two to summarize the context of verse 13. Discuss the following:

- In the first century, what did the saying "to live like a Corinthian" mean?
- Hamilton contends that this passage is not about facing adversity and the difficult circumstances of life, but about something else. What is it?
- Paul tells the Corinthians that their experience of being tempted is not unique. What does Paul say about the experience of temptation—for the Corinthians and for us?

Book Study and Discussion

Exploring Temptation

Invite a volunteer to describe the example of temptation given by the writer. Then ask other volunteers to give examples of temptations they have faced—and perhaps are facing—by completing this open-ended prompt:

- Temptation comes to me in the form of…

If participants choose to respond with more lighthearted examples of temptation, similar to Hamilton's example of being tempted by a rolling cart of food, encourage them to reflect in silence on what temptations in their own lives represent more profound challenges to faithful living.

Discuss:

- Hamilton contends that it is not God who tempts us. Do you agree or disagree? Why?
- He also observes that God tries to put up speed bumps and roadblocks to remind us that we're on the road to temptation and it is time to choose a different path. Has this been your experience? If so, can you describe what the result was?

Revisit the opening activity, in which the group considered the helpfulness of the statement "God won't give you more than you can handle." Invite them to consider the veracity of that statement by examining the first part of it—that is, when we experience things that are difficult to handle, do they come from God?

Examine the Half Truth and the Better Promise

Review with the group their exploration in Session 1 of the idea that suffering comes from God. Hamilton observes that the saying for this session is related to that idea. Invite volunteers to describe Hamilton's examples of the myriad difficult circumstances faced by people in Malawi and of the note he received from a woman in his congregation.

Distribute the copies of news accounts that you used in Session 1, as well as any updated accounts of events that have happened since that session. Ask participants to read over these news accounts. Discuss some of the following:

- Do you believe that God gave people the horrible, painful, hurtful experiences in the news accounts or the examples of such experiences from your own life? If God didn't cause them, how do you account for them?
- Insurance companies label natural disasters (and some other events that result in damage to property and loss of

life) as "acts of God." Would you say the events you've been discussing are acts of God? If not, what would be a better way to describe them?

- The words of Scripture don't say that bad things will not happen to us. What do the words of Scripture affirm instead?

Invite someone to read aloud the second focus scripture, Psalm 46:1-2 (found above and at the beginning of book Chapter 3). Refer the group to the story in the text about the woman whose son committed suicide in front of her. Invite group members to discuss the following:

- Three years after her son's suicide, the woman posted a note on Facebook telling how she had survived this trauma with God's help. What does she mean when she refers to "stretcher bearers"? (If that term does not ring a bell for the group, refer them to the story of the man lowered through the roof, found in Matthew 9:1-8; Mark 2:1-12; and Luke 5:17-26.) Who have been your stretcher bearers in times of trauma and sorrow?
- Though he might experience the pain of a traumatic event for the rest of his life, Hamilton maintains faith that, at some point, joy will overshadow pain. Have you found this to be true in your own life experiences?
- How would you define what the prophet Zechariah calls "prisoners of hope"?

In the book, a woman wrote her pastor that she would lose it if one more person told her God would not give her more than she could handle. The woman went on to affirm that God was helping her cope, and she listed ways in which she could give thanks to God. Encourage group members in the coming week to evaluate their own experiences of loss, pain, and trauma. Ask them to use their journals to do what the woman was doing—affirming that God is helping them cope, and listing ways of giving thanks to God as they journey toward healing.

More Activities (Optional)

Consider Idols that Tempt

Review the information Hamilton tells us about the context for Paul's first letter to the church at Corinth. Ask volunteers to describe what temptations the Christians at Corinth were facing. Say that the problem for the Corinthians was the same problem Paul noted had faced the Israelites: giving in to idol worship. Ask:

- How would you define idolatry?
- What idols tempt us today in our context?

Ask participants to think further about today's idols—that is, objects, attitudes, and practices on which we rely and sometimes place (or misplace) our allegiance—and list those idols on a board or a large sheet of paper.

Distribute drawing paper and colored markers or crayons. Invite participants to choose one idol that tempts them. Ask them to use symbols, words, or phrases to depict this idol. After allowing time for them to work, ask each person to explain their idol to the group. Then ask participants to reflect on pathways God provides to help us resist the temptation of idolatry. Encourage them to continue reflecting on and praying about how to resist these temptations with God's help.

Create Poetry

Invite group members to read over the story of Annie Johnson Flint in the text. Have them name the various challenges and adversities faced by Flint during her lifetime. Ask a volunteer to read aloud the poem "What God Hath Promised."

On a board or a large sheet of paper, print the following open-ended prompts: "What God has promised…" and "What God has not promised…" Invite participants, using their journals, to write words or phrases in response to each prompt. After allowing time for participants to reflect and write, invite them to call out some of the words or phrases they chose. Record these on the paper or board under the appropriate prompt. Read all the responses for each prompt aloud as a group poem.

Experience the Lord's Prayer

On a large sheet of paper or a board, print the following words from the Lord's Prayer (Matthew 6:9-13 KJV): "Lead us not into temptation, but deliver us from evil." Hamilton points out that this sentence might need an additional comma. Print his suggested version: "Lead us, not into temptation, but deliver us from evil."

Invite someone to describe how the meaning is transformed with the comma added. Invite the group to consider what things in their own lives tempt them away from God's path. Then ask them to join in saying the Lord's Prayer together. Encourage them, as they pray, to ask God's help in avoiding temptation.

Wrapping Up

Closing Activity

Remind the group that in the opening activity, you read aloud some words from the text that people often say, with the best of intentions, to those enduring painful experiences. Ask participants to think about what they would like to hear in a situation like that. Then read the following passages aloud, and invite group members to complete the passages with words of comfort that might be more helpful by acknowledging the person's pain and offering an affirmation of God's help.

> I know you're going through a tough time right now. You feel like you're sinking. The burden is too heavy. You don't know how much more you can bear...

Then read aloud the second focus scripture (Psalm 46:1-2), followed by the passage from Romans 8 that was mentioned in the book:

> Who will separate us from Christ's love? Will we be separated by trouble, or distress, or harassment, or famine, or nakedness, or danger, or sword?...But in all these things we win a sweeping victory through the one who loved us. I'm convinced that nothing can separate us from God's love in Christ Jesus our Lord: not death or life, not angels or rulers, not present things or future things, not powers or height or depth, or any other thing that is created. (Romans 8:35, 37-39)

Remind group members to read Chapter 4 before the next session.

Closing Prayer

Offer the following prayer that ends Chapter 3:

O God, how grateful we are for the way you walk with us in every moment of our lives. In those moments when we're tempted and tested, help us remember that we can resist and that you make a way out of temptation. You give us the strength we need when we turn to you. Lead us, not into temptation as we would go, but in your path and away from evil.

When we walk through difficulty and adversity, help us remember that these burdens did not come from you, but that you have said you would help us bear them. Thank you for people who come along our path and help carry us through those challenging times. Help us have eyes to see those around us who need your help—and to see how we might be instruments of your help for them. How grateful we are, O God, that you are our refuge and strength, an ever-present help in times of trouble. Therefore we will not fear, even when our world seems to be falling apart. Amen.

4.

GOD SAID IT, I BELIEVE IT, THAT SETTLES IT

Planning the Session

Session Goals

As a result of conversations and activities connected with this session, group members should begin to:

- examine the ways this half truth does not capture the truth of the Bible;
- embrace an understanding of the Bible as a complex document that must be interpreted, using the teachings of Jesus as the standard against which all scriptures must be measured.

Biblical Foundation

You shall have a designated area outside the camp to which you shall go. With your utensils you shall have a trowel; when you relieve yourself outside, you shall dig a hole with it and then cover up your excrement. Because the LORD your God travels along with your camp, to save you and to hand over your enemies to you, therefore your camp must be holy, so that he may not see anything indecent among you and turn away from you.

—*Deuteronomy 23:12-14 NRSV*

Special Preparation

- Christians approach the Bible's origins and meanings from a variety of perspectives, so in this session you'll need to be particularly aware of and sensitive to people's views. Keep in mind that for some participants, it may be quite challenging to consider any explanation that deviates from direct dictation from God or to consider that there may be contradictions within Scripture.
- If you are unsure that participants will have Internet access during group time to search for the bumper sticker "God said it, I believe it, that settles it," do a search yourself in advance of the session and print some examples of bumper stickers.
- If possible, bring a colander for the activity called "Explore an Analogy," in which Jesus' words are used as a standard for evaluating other scriptures.
- If you decide to do one of the optional activities, gather the necessary materials. For "Design Bumper Stickers," you will need posterboard or card stock cut into rectangular strips 11.50-by-3.75 inches, as well as pencils and colored markers. You might also cut white self-stick shelf liner into pieces of those dimensions. Or if you like, plan to point the group to a site like http://www.customink.com/styles/115-x-375 -rectangular-bumper-sticker/106900, where they can design a bumper sticker online. For the other two optional activities, all you will need is a large sheet of paper or a board and markers, and writing paper or participants' journals and pens.

Getting Started

Opening Activity

Welcome group members, and introduce any who are new to the group. Gather together. Invite group members with Internet access to search online for the statement "God said it, I believe it, that settles it." Try to find bumper stickers with the slogan and its variations. Ask:

- What do you think this bumper sticker is trying to convey?
- Would you put this bumper sticker on your car? Why or why not?

Tell the group that in this session, they will examine whether this statement represents biblical truth, and if not, how one arrives at the Bible's deeper and more complex truth.

Opening Prayer

Pray the following, or a prayer of your choosing:

Holy God, we give thanks that through the words of the Bible, you speak a Word to us. Guide us as together we seek to discern your will for our lives. In the name of Jesus Christ we pray. Amen.

Learning Together

Video Study and Discussion

Adam Hamilton explores a half truth that is perhaps less familiar to many: "God said it, I believe it, that settles it." Hamilton discusses how this statement can come to shape someone's expression of faith.

- Hamilton suggests that when we talk about "inspiration," there are many different ways of defining how God speaks to the biblical authors. How would you explain the inspiration of Scripture? How do you respond to the idea that the ways biblical writers were inspired by God differed from writer to writer?

- What does Hamilton have to say about the translation of Scripture? What factors come into play that might influence how a passage is translated? What questions does a translator need to ask? What questions do we, the readers of Scripture, need to ask?

Bible Study and Discussion

Tell the group that in all probability, this session is the first time—and likely the last time—that they will study today's focus passage, Deuteronomy 23:12–14. Ask a volunteer to read it aloud. (The passage can be found above and at the beginning of book Chapter 4.) Tell the group that this passage is part of a section of the Law that lays out sanitary, ritual, and humanitarian precepts. Give the context described in the chapter: The Israelites were in the wilderness prior to entering the Promised Land. God was dwelling in their midst, and in order that God not witness anything deemed indecent, such as human elimination, the people were enjoined to go outside their encampment to relieve themselves. Discuss:

- Adam Hamilton tells us that in the 1880s, sermons were preached on this passage. Why?
- Ask the group to name more recent inventions and suggest ways in which today's preachers may be interpreting Scripture to discuss these.

Book Study and Discussion

Examine Anachronisms in Scripture

Call the group's attention to the list of prohibitions under the heading "Going to Extremes" in Hamilton's book. Invite participants to read the list of ways we would need to alter our lives if indeed we were serious about "God said it, I believe it, that settles it." Ask each person to name one item on this list that represents something they would have to change in their own lives.

Explore Interpretation on Two Issues

Point out that some issues discussed in the Bible, such the sanitary rules in this week's focus scripture, may be related to customs of the time rather than to deep and enduring truths. Two important issues that may fall into this category are the treatment of women and the institution of slavery. Form two smaller groups, one to discuss women in the Bible and the other to discuss slavery. Ask each group to read the information in book Chapter 4 about their issue and be prepared to cite examples of what the Bible has to say about it, as well as the context for such statements and any information in the Bible that seems to contradict the statements. Back in the large group, ask each smaller group to report what they found. Discuss some of the following:

- Where and why does Paul seem to be contradicting himself with respect to the role of women?
- How do you respond to the suggestion that Paul was trying to calm things down in the face of controversy resulting from the greater equality of women in the early church? Does this seem to be a reasonable explanation for the apparent contradictions in what Paul said about women, or can you think of other plausible explanations?
- How did advocates of slavery in the United States interpret scriptures that addressed slavery?
- Nowhere in Scripture is there categorical condemnation of human slavery. Why do you think this is so?

Examine the Half Truth in "God Said It"

Point out that "God said it, I believe it, that settles it" is a less-than-ideal way for Christians to read Scripture, because it focuses on a half truth rather than helping persons to seek the deeper truth. On a large sheet of paper or a board, print the following:

> Every word of the Bible was dictated by God and recorded by the hands of human writers.

Invite volunteers to respond to this understanding of how the Bible came to be. Point out Adam Hamilton's contention that this does not accurately reflect how Scripture was written.

Discuss some of the following together:

- Paul uses a word that does not seem to appear in the Greek language: *theopneustos*. What is the literal meaning of the word? How might we interpret the word with respect to the way Scripture was written?
- How does our understanding of the way our Bible was written differ from what Muslims believe about the Qur'an?
- What does Paul contend is the purpose of Scripture?
- In what ways does Scripture function for you? How do you experience God speaking to you through Scripture?

Examine the Half Truth of "That Settles It"

Invite a volunteer to read aloud the first paragraph under the heading "The Problem with 'That Settles It.'" Form pairs. Ask one person in each pair to read the book information under this heading related to Jesus and his interpretation of Scripture, while the other person reads about Paul and the controversy over circumcision. Ask the members of each pair to discuss interpretation and context of Scripture. After allowing a few minutes for pairs to exchange ideas, discuss some of the following together in the large group:

- What are some times when Jesus interpreted the Scriptures in new ways?
- Based on your reading of the book and the Bible, what was Jesus inviting his listeners—and us—to do?
- What was the controversy among the apostles of the early church regarding circumcision? Why did Paul preach that the law on circumcision no longer applied?
- Paul was a Pharisee who was rigorously schooled in the Law, and yet he parted from the Law in the case of circumcision. Why do you think he did so, and what does it tell us about Paul's beliefs?

Explore an Analogy

Under the book's Chapter 4 heading "The Definitive Word of God," Hamilton offers some guidelines for interpreting Scripture, including Bible commentaries, study Bibles, and conversations with trusted pastors and friends. Discuss these guidelines, as well as other guidelines suggested by group members.

Hamilton points out that, for him, there is an even more important lens for interpretation: the life and words of Jesus. Call the group's attention to the colander you brought to class, and ask how Jesus' life and words can serve as a kind of colander for interpreting the Bible. Discuss:

- What are some examples from Scripture that, measured against Jesus' life and words, we might choose to let pass? What are some examples that are affirmed by Jesus' life and words?
- We read about A. J. Jacobs, author of the book *The Year of Living Biblically*. After living a year attempting to follow the Bible as literally as possible, what did Jacobs conclude? What do you think of his conclusion?

- Hamilton, while stressing the importance of Bible interpretation, notes the danger in picking and choosing Scripture. What is that danger? Do you agree? Can you think of other dangers in doing so?

More Activities (Optional)

Design Bumper Stickers

In our society, T-shirts are like billboards where people express ideas and philosophies. Bumper stickers function in the same way, allowing people to express philosophical positions as they drive around. Invite group members to consider what they might put on a bumper sticker that would express how they interpret Scripture.

Distribute the prepared card stock, poster board, or self-stick shelf liner strips and markers. Encourage participants to formulate their ideas on scratch paper, then allow time for them to show their ideas to others for suggestions and critique. As suggested in "Special Preparation," you may alternatively point the group to the suggested website where they can design a bumper sticker online.

When participants have finished their bumper stickers, allow time for each person to explain their creation to the group. If you chose to take the next step and have the group design T-shirts, distribute drawing paper and pencils and follow the same process with participants to develop designs.

Create New Analogies

Invite participants to generate popcorn-style other possible analogies (besides a colander) for using the life and words of Jesus as the standard for evaluating other scriptures. Print their suggestions on a large sheet of paper or a board. Then choose two or three of the suggested analogies and form smaller groups to flesh them out.

Allow time for the smaller groups to develop the analogies as fully as possible, then come together in the large group to report and discuss each one.

Formulate Questions for Jesus and Paul

Form two groups. Assign one group to consider how Paul interpreted Scripture and to the other group how Jesus interpreted Scripture. Ask each group to read over information under the heading "The Problem with 'That Settles It'" that is relevant to their assignment. Then ask them to assume the characters of Pharisees and religious leaders (in the case of Jesus) or Jewish Christians (in the case of Paul) and formulate questions they would ask Jesus or Paul about why and how they rely on interpretation and context. After allowing time for each group to generate a list of questions, have them read their questions in the large group. Discuss how Jesus and Paul might have answered the questions.

Wrapping Up

Closing Activity

Invite participants to make observations or raise lingering questions about the half truth "God said it, I believe it, that settles it."

Point out that the Bible is a testimony of its authors to their faith in and experience with God and God's will. It is our defining story. Through Scripture we can hear God speak. As a result, reading the Bible becomes a means of grace.

Read aloud Paul's words in 2 Timothy 3:16-17.

> Every scripture is inspired by God and is useful for teaching, for showing mistakes, for correcting, and for training character, so that the person who belongs to God can be equipped to do everything that is good.

Encourage participants to be open to ways in which God may be speaking to them through Scripture in the coming week. As they experience the Bible, ask that they keep in mind how the life and words of Jesus Christ can help them interpret what they read.

Remind group members to read Chapter 5 before the next session.

5.

LOVE THE SINNER, HATE THE SIN

Planning the Session

Session Goals

As a result of conversations and activities connected with this session, group members should begin to:

- examine the ways that this half truth does not capture the truth of the Bible;
- embrace the understanding that we are called to live under the reign of love.

Biblical Foundation

[Jesus said to them,] "Don't judge, so that you won't be judged. You'll receive the same judgment you give. Whatever you deal out

*will be dealt out to you. Why do you see the splinter that's in your
brother's or sister's eye, but don't notice the log in your own eye?
How can you say to your brother or sister, 'Let me take the splinter
out of your eye,' when there's a log in your eye? You deceive yourself!
First take the log out of your eye, and then you'll see clearly to take
the splinter out of your brother's or sister's eye."*

—Matthew 7:1-5

Special Preparation

- Decide if you will do either of the optional activities. If you
  choose to do the activity "Consider Questions," print the
  questions on a large sheet of paper or a board and post it.
- For the closing activity of this final session, print each of the
  five book chapter titles on a separate large sheet of paper and
  post the sheets at intervals around your learning space. Next
  to each sheet, place a black marker and one other marker of a
  different color.

Getting Started

Opening Activity

Welcome group members to this final session in the study. Tell the
group that today's session addresses the half truth "Love the sinner,
hate the sin." Call for a show of hands for those who have recently
heard someone say these words. Ask:

- What was the situation in which you heard someone say
  this?
- What was your impression of the speaker's intentions? What
  was your impression of the effect?

A second statement often accompanies this half truth: "No sin is worse than any other." This second statement is usually spoken by well-intended Christians. Yet Adam Hamilton tells us that neither statement is biblical. In this session, participants will have the opportunity to examine both statements, words that may come across as anything but loving to those to whom they are directed.

Opening Prayer

Loving God, we come to you as sinners in need of forgiveness. Be with us today as together we explore your Word, that we may discern what it means to live under the reign of love. In the name of Jesus Christ, who showed us what your love is like. Amen.

Learning Together

Video Study and Discussion

Adam Hamilton explores a statement often heard in church circles today: "Love the sinner, hate the sin." He discusses ways in which this statement is biblically sound and ways in which it is biblically off the mark.

- If this statement were directed at you, how would it make you feel? Does it come across as helpful? Do you feel defensive?
- If you have observed this statement being made to another person, how do you think that person felt? What are some other things that could have been said instead?
- Would you say that all sins are equal? Give some contrasting examples of sins that are not equal.
- What sin does Hamilton tell us is considered the worst by Catholics? Why?

Bible Study and Discussion

Invite a volunteer to read aloud today's focus scripture, Matthew 7:1–5. (The scripture can be found above and at the beginning of book Chapter 5.) Remind the group that this passage is part of what is called the Sermon on the Mount, in which Jesus is preaching to a large crowd. Ask:

- What is Jesus' point here about spiritual blindness and judging others?
- Hamilton observes that if he were going to sum up Jesus' meaning in this passage, it would not be "Love the sinner, hate the sin" but something else altogether. What does he suggest it would be? What do you think it would be?

Book Study and Discussion

Exploring the Definition of Sin

Invite volunteers to give the meaning of both the Hebrew word *chata*, the word for sin used in the Old Testament, and *hamartia*, the Greek word for sin most commonly used in the New Testament.

To explore whether all sins are equal, ask participants to name, popcorn style, various acts that they would consider to be sin across the whole spectrum of severity. Jot these down on a board or a large sheet of paper. Invite the group to read over the variety of sins named, from the relatively trivial to those most would consider heinous. Then ask:

- When we look at Jesus' words in the Sermon on the Mount, it may appear that he says contemplating a sin and actually committing a sin are the same thing, but in fact that is not the case. What does Adam Hamilton indicate Jesus is saying? What do you think?

- In the focus Scripture, what do you believe Jesus is calling us to do?
- What does Hamilton mean when he says we are meant to take Jesus' words seriously, not literally?
- What do Roman Catholics mean by the distinction between venial sins and mortal sins? Do you agree with this categorization? Why or why not?

Invite the group to name what Catholics identify as the capital sins—often referred to as the Seven Deadly Sins. Discuss:

- Why do Catholics identify these as deadly?
- Which of these seven "root" sins is considered by Catholics as more deadly and dangerous than any of the others? Why?

Examine the Words "Love the Sinner"

Hamilton notes that the first part of this week's half truth, "Love the sinner," is true as far as it goes, but it doesn't go quite far enough. Discuss some of the following together:

- Jesus never actually says, "Love the sinner." What does he say instead?
- Hamilton observes that loving people as neighbors doesn't necessarily mean having warm feelings for them, or even liking them personally. What does it mean to love our neighbors?
- Why are we to love our enemies especially?
- Hamilton suggests there are two reasons why Jesus never said "Love the sinner," the first being that it would be redundant since the neighbor and the enemy are both sinners. What is the second reason?
- Do you find yourself labeling people as sinners who engage in behavior you consider sinful? How does that affect the way you interact with them?

- How does Jesus define *neighbor*? How do you define it?
- How does Hamilton sum up Jesus' message? How would you?

Examine the words "Hate the Sin"

Hamilton tells us that, for him, the stumbling block in the phrase "Hate the sin" is the word *hate*. Invite group members to give examples of the kinds of people Jesus seemed to seek out. Discuss some of the following:

- When Jesus speaks to sinners, he never seems to bring up the subject of sin but rather speaks of something else. What is it? How do you feel about this?
- With respect to sin, what is it that Jesus wants us to recognize?

Form pairs. Assign to one person in each pair the information given in the book about the woman caught in adultery, also referring them to the scriptural account in John 8:1–11. Assign to the other person the information in the book about Jesus denouncing some of the religious leaders, also referring them to the scriptural account in Matthew 23:13–36. Allow the pairs to read and discuss their assignments. Back in the large group, ask:

- What is Jesus' attitude toward the woman taken in adultery and toward her sin? What do his words and actions indicate about how he regards her?
- What do Jesus' words to the religious leaders indicate about his attitude toward them?
- Hamilton notes that of course we should not keep silent about the problem of sin. What sort of sin does he contend we must hate and denounce? What distinctions do you make among various sins?

More Activities (Optional)

Step into the Story

Invite the group to explore the parable of the Pharisee and the tax collector. In order to understand these two characters as polar opposites, ask group members to read the description in the book about each man. Also refer them to the scriptural account in Luke 18:9–14. Then ask two volunteers to take the parts of the Pharisee and the tax collector, reading their words from the Bible and taking on the attitudes and postures suggested by the passage. Invite the remaining participants to take the role of bystanders who observe the two men praying in the Temple. After hearing the two men pray, ask the men to describe what their predominant emotions and attitudes about themselves were. Then ask participants to discuss the following:

- As you heard these two men praying, what opinions did you form about them?
- In all honesty, with which man do you identify the most?
- How do you think the Pharisee would view other people he considers sinners? How would the tax collector view them?
- Would you say that you tend to disassociate yourself from certain types of people? Why or why not?

Consider Questions

Hamilton observes that these days he most often hears "Love the sinner, hate the sin" in the context of a discussion on homosexuality. He notes that the Bible contains a handful of passages from Moses and Paul that indicate disapproval of some form of same-sex practice. He lists the following questions, all of which are pertinent, for consideration and reflection:

- How do Moses' and Paul's words capture God's view of his gay and lesbian children? Do these verses capture God's will for all time?
- Do the Moses and Paul passages speak to the way God wants us to live today, or were they more the products of a particular context?
- Were they even addressing the same things we talk about today when we think of same-sex relationships? Did these ancient writers understand things such as sexual orientation?
- To what extent do you feel that the Moses and Paul passages are parallel to the Bible passages on the subjugation of women and slaves? That is, is it possible these passages are more an expression of the cultural context than the will of God?

Distribute writing paper and pens, or ask participants to record their responses in their journals. Then read each of the above questions, and ask people to choose one of the following responses: "Yes, I agree"; "No, I disagree"; or "I would like to get more information or explore further."

When everyone has had a chance to respond, encourage participants to reflect further on the questions in the coming weeks. Discuss:

- Regardless of our views on these questions, how do you think we can demonstrate Christ's love to LGBT persons and those who love and support them, without resorting to the language and actions of "Love the sinner, hate the sin"?
- Hamilton recounts Billy Graham's comments to his daughter about his interaction with the Clintons. In your opinion, how do we best demonstrate love in situations such as this?
- Hamilton also tells the story of a note that a visiting gay couple received from one of the congregants in the

church. If you had been writing that note, what would you have said?

Wrapping Up

Closing Activity

Invite group members to reflect in their journals in the coming week on the following:

- How do I show God's love to my neighbors?
- How do I avoid convicting or judging others, trusting that the Holy Spirit is at work in their lives just as the Spirit works in me?

Call the group's attention to the five chapter titles in this study, each recorded on a large sheet of paper. Form five smaller groups or pairs and send each pair or group to one of the posted sheets. For each topic, ask participants to review the session's discussion as they remember it. Then have them use the black marker to write any comments, and use the colored marker to pose questions they still have and might like to pursue later. The groups or pairs should then move to the next sheet and write comments and questions there as well.

When each group or pair has had a chance to address every topic, come together in the large group. Ask volunteers to give their thoughts and feelings about the study as a whole. Encourage participants to continue reflecting on what they have learned and to pray for further discernment. Then invite the group to respond to the following open-ended prompt:

- When I am in a situation where I am tempted to say (fill in one of the half truths), I will respond in this way instead...

Closing Prayer

Offer the following prayer, which ends Chapter 5.

Lord Jesus, how grateful we are that you came not to show judgment to sinners, but to offer forgiveness to us; not to point out all our sins, but to show the way and the truth and the life. How grateful we are that you continue to save us from our sins; that you forgive us and show us mercy; and that you have called us who have received mercy to give mercy. Help us to be the kind of followers who welcome people and love them in your name. Help us to live that life of love not just in church but in our lives every day. In your holy name. Amen.

ABOUT THE VIDEOS

The videos in this program were filmed at Thistle Stop Café, part of the Thistle Farms ministry in Nashville. Thistle Farms is a powerful community of women who have survived prostitution, trafficking, and addiction. The ministry includes a two-year residential program and advocacy services for up to 700 women yearly. Adam Hamilton's congregation, The United Methodist Church of the Resurrection, supports Healing House, a faith-based substance abuse recovery organization in the Kansas City metropolitan area for men and women who are committed to becoming responsible, productive, drug- and alcohol-free community members. We celebrate the healing power of love in our communities.

CPSIA information can be obtained
at www.ICGtesting.com
Printed in the USA
LVOW12s0957081016
507739LV00005BA/5/P